Connie
Many Blessings

Author: Yassin S. Hall | Co-Author: Loán C. Sewer

JOURNEY UNTOLD

TWISTED LOVE

MY MOTHER'S STRUGGLE WITH MENTAL ILLNESS

JOURNEY UNTOLD: TWISTED LOVE –
MY MOTHER'S STRUGGLE WITH MENTAL ILLNESS

JOURNEY UNTOLD

TWISTED LOVE

MY MOTHER'S STRUGGLE WITH MENTAL ILLNESS

YASSIN S. HALL

AS TOLD TO LOÁN C. SEWER

JOURNEY UNTOLD: TWISTED LOVE –
MY MOTHER'S STRUGGLE WITH MENTAL ILLNESS

PRAISE FOR JOURNEY UNTOLD

"Journey Untold" is poignant, captivating, stirring - - a deeply emotional story of a child's journey with a mother who suffered from mental illness. Ms. Hall has opened the window of her soul and allows us to experience the deep, personal truths of everyday life with a parent who is mentally ill. This is not an ordinary story. Nothing prepares a young child for the twists, turns, volatility, triumphs and defeats of watching a parent's mind slowly disintegrate. Living in a small community many, like me, personally witnessed some of her experiences. Journey Untold boldly exposes and confronts mental illness. It is page turning, twisted with emotions, truthful and agonizing; but in the end, "every little thing is going to be alright." (Bob Marely's Three Little Birds) - Julie S. Carr

It was very informative, touching and sad at the same time. I used to see your mother all the time and I knew something was wrong. I always wondered why no one would try to help her, like family or friends. I have an aunt and a cousin in Tortola who have the same disease. At the [book] reading my eyes were opened on mental illness and how to tell the different signs and effects it has on people. You are truly blessed and strong Yassin to grow up dealing with your mother's illness and your family issues. I am proud of you that you wrote this book about your life experiences to share with people and educate those of us who don't know about schizophrenia. Love ya! - Dwayne Harley

Yassin Hall exposes the wounds of her past in the book <u>Journey Untold.</u> She offers a glimpse into a mind in turmoil, exploring the physical aspects of mental illness and providing insight into the chaos that lies beneath the surface. Today she wants others to know that they, too, can enjoy relief and peace. This book is beautifully written, heartwarming, touching insights, a book with a Powerful message. Whether you are the partner, parents, friend, or child of a depressed person, you'll find this book an invaluable companion in your "Journey" back to health. - Walden Maduro

The pleasure was mine to have the opportunity to engage in the presentation of Yassin Hall's book <u>Journey Untold</u>. My awareness relating to mentally ill individuals has become apparent. Yassin's book is a wonderful read that will assist in educating our world about this unfortunate illness.

- Magarita Harris

"If I can motivate, empower, and uplift
just one woman a day, then that's my purpose.
That is what keeps me going." – Yassin S. Hall

JOURNEY UNTOLD: TWISTED LOVE –
MY MOTHER'S STRUGGLE WITH MENTAL ILLNESS

Copyright © 2014 Yassin S. Hall

ISBN:1502927268
ISBN-13: 978-1502927262

DEDICATION

This book is dedicated to my mother, Vernice Simmonds (Rest in Peace); my father, Victor Hall (Rest in Peace); my uncle, Samuel H. Hall, Jr.; and my grandmother, Delia Simmonds.

CONTENTS

INTRODUCTION

What is it about mental illness that makes people just act like it doesn't exist? Despite strides made today, it is not openly discussed in many communities, especially in communities of color, like the one I grew up in, in the U.S. Virgin Islands. Whether in the U.S., the Caribbean, Africa, our South America, there is still a lot of shame associated with mental illness, so people choose often to suffer silently while their lives are unraveling right in front of their eyes.

This memoir offers a look at mental illness from my perspective as the child of a mother suffering from the effects of schizophrenia. The pages ahead offer a snapshot of the early years of my life, the beginning of my "Journey Untold," and my journey to finding myself. In it, you will hear an honest, first-person narrative of the early years that shaped the woman I am today, and from time to time, "Self," the outspoken part of my personality may share a thought or two. No, I don't have split personalities, but it's just my way of giving you all of me, as authentically and openly as I know how.

A few years ago I embarked on a journey to develop a women's clothing line and that opened the door for some amazing opportunities. One of them was to host my spring collection fashion show every year in March to showcase the latest designs to potential customers. During my 2014 "Spring into a New YOU" fashion showcase, I made the decision to share a little about myself with the attendees and provide them with a look into the heart and soul of the person creating and selling these fashions for them. It was life-changing. By the time I finished sharing my story with them, there was not a dry eye in the room, and after the show people were coming up to me saying how my words had touched them. So here we are today, with *Journey Untold*. It is a raw, unapologetic perspective – from *my* point of view - of the period in my childhood when I lost my mother to the sneaky, unsuspecting grip of mental illness and what that experience did to and for me.

My hope is that this book will help to remove the shame associated with this disease and that a discussion can take place in personal circles about the harm that is done when we keep silent about unpopular disorders for fear of shame, retribution, or bullying. Mental illness is real; its consequences are soul shattering; and the lives left to pick up the pieces can only be rebuilt with truth and acceptance.

Ms. Yassy

PROLOGUE

Life is a journey. One that can make us laugh, make us cry, or hell, just make or break us. I should know! This life of mine has definitely been unforgettable and has made me bawl my eyes out, want to throw bricks at folks, and, if I can be brutally honest, made me wish I could just escape. But through it all, I've had my two people in my life who have been the glue that has helped me keep it all together, my maternal grandmother, Delia Simmonds and my paternal uncle Samuel H. Hall, Jr. In truth, they were the only family I really had until I had my own. I've always heard that you shouldn't envy people because you don't know what they've gone through to get to where they are in life. Ain't that the truth? I tend to post a lot of my life's moments on social media, so people see me running my businesses and doing things with my children and assume that I have not a care in the world. Well, you know what they say about assuming, right? If they only know the things I've experienced to become the woman I am today, they'd probably bolt in the other direction.

You see, I am the daughter of someone who lost herself to the devastating effects of mental illness. However, her disease didn't just affect her — it cheated me out of all the special occurrences that define childhood and robbed my grandparents of a life with their daughter, my mom, Vernice. I'll never forget the day that I lost my mom for the first time and began to understand that something was very wrong. I was twelve years old, and it was a day that would change my world forever. Little did I know this would be the start of totally unscripted, vast experiences that now are my 'Journey Untold.'

CHAPTER ONE

It's amazing the things that the heart and mind can endure. No one ever told me that growing up, so I often spent my childhood thinking something was wrong with me. For most of my life I have felt as though I wasn't wanted, wasn't welcome, and that something was wrong with me. I could never quite put my finger on it, but I didn't quite belong. Can any of you relate to that?

In order for you to understand me and my story, I think I should tell you a little bit about where I am from. I was born and raised on the Caribbean island of St. Thomas, in the U.S. Virgin Islands. That's about thirty minutes away from Puerto Rico, if you need a better frame of reference. The Virgin Islands is a territory of the United States so we are U.S. citizens by birth, operate under the U.S. governmental laws and systems, but we are a part of the Caribbean with a heritage that goes back to being once owned by Denmark as the Danish West Indies until 1917. The U.S. Virgin Islands consists of St. Thomas, St. John, St. Croix, and Water Island, along with hundreds of other inlets and cays.

St. Thomas is tiny; just thirty-two square miles and the entire population is about 50,000-55,000 people. So if you can imagine my childhood, it was a very small community where everyone knew your parents, grandparents, great-grandparents and so on. That said, when you have a member of your family with mental illness, it's a bit hard to hide, especially when everyone knows that the affected person is related to you. In this setting, it would prove difficult to come to terms with the life that had haunted me and left me feeling like I was stained and unworthy of love.

It was early in my childhood when I realized that my mom wasn't like the other parents. I didn't have a close relationship with my father, Victor Hall, at the time, but I spent a lot of time growing up with my mother's parents. My mom, Vernice, was rather quiet; more of an introvert. Well…that was all before our world started to unravel. My parents were high school sweethearts who courted in secret from ninth to twelve grade. Their courtship continued into college and I was the end result of their young romance. Sounds sweet, huh? Well I thought so too, however, as I've started to put all the pieces together in the past few years, it's becoming much clearer that there was trouble brewing in paradise.

My mother and father had an on again, off again relationship after high school, but during their courtship, marriage was on both of their minds – at least for a little while. My father even proposed to her, but she surprised him and everyone else by telling him she would not marry him. My grandmother wasn't even aware that they had been dating so seriously. I guess they did a great job of convincing her and everyone else that they had met in their first year of college at the University of the Virgin Islands (UVI).

The real story is that they were sneaking around to avoid dealing with their parents' opinions and my mother would hop on the boat to St. John a few times a year to see my dad outside of the school day. They were both twenty or twenty-one years of age when I was born and whatever was going on in their relationship, my father was missing in action for my mother's pregnancy. How awful for her. She was pregnant with her first child for the man who was supposed to be the love of her life, and then when she needed him the most he just up and left. *I'm shaking my damn head at how conveniently he just disappeared from the scene, but I'm not going to be bitter. Now back to the story.*

My father must have come to his senses that day and went to ask my mom to come back to him. How ironic that while he was standing on my grandmother's doorstep, Mommy was in the hospital preparing to bring me into the world. Given that I too was a young mother, I can only imagine how scary that must have been. The long and short of the story is that after my birth, things were never quite the same. Looking back now, I think my mother knew that she would not be able to care for me in an adequate manner, so she went about making provisions to ensure that I would be in good hands. In a secret conversation with her aunt and uncle, she arranged for them to take me in as an infant. I'm not sure why she didn't have this talk with her own parents but that was her decision…no lawyers or fancy talk, just a verbal agreement that they would raise me.

She had worked everything out unofficially for them to become my guardians and then just like that, my dad came back on the scene and said he was taking me to St. John to go live with his parents. As I said my parents had discussed getting married so this was during their on-again period and they were going to be together.

8

However, something triggered in her mind, and she immediately changed her mind and returned to St. Thomas to once again place me with my great-aunt and great-uncle. Had folks been connecting the dots they would have realized that something was a bit off with my mother, but at the time no one could piece together that something was very wrong. *I mean, who just hands over their newborn without any hesitation?*

By the time I was five years old, I had been bounced around between my relatives on St. Thomas and St. John – my great-aunt and uncle; my mom's parents; and my father's mother. All the while, my dad was not really in the picture. No wonder I would later feel like a freak. I mean, what was so bad about me that my own parents didn't want me around? Was I stained with something unforgiveable? These were just some of the questions that I would later ask myself, and I now see how this shaped the majority of the first half of my life.

Ultimately, I wound up back with my maternal grandparents, Mama and Eric – that's what I called my grandparents – and I found a little piece of normalcy until the other telltale signs of my mother's illness began to spring forth. After having me, Mommy found her own places to live and was living off of Section 8 benefits. At the time, this was not something you wanted other people to know but she had her own apartment in different parts of the island so she appeared capable of being on her own – or so we thought.

There were little signs here and there – at least that's what Mama has told me; however, if I can go back a bit, you'll see that my mother once was what the world calls "normal." She was rather intelligent, and was working with the local health department and social welfare agency right out of high school before she attended college. Everyone who worked with her knew she was an excellent typist, a skill that earned her rave reviews from the head of the agencies during her brief tenure with each department.

What's most interesting is that my mother was working for agencies that helped others to get their health and their livelihood together, yet unbeknownst to all of us, her sanity and welfare were gradually slipping away. How ironic, given the way our lives would turn out, that she got her start helping others with their social welfare. I guess God has a strange sense of humor. Though Mommy lived on a different part of the island, she would come and get me from my grandmother's house each morning to take me to school after Mama got me ready; and then things changed. I noticed it one day out of the blue when we were both in the house and later on, when I was coming home from school. I thought, *"Why is my mom speaking a funny language that no one could understand? And why for God's sake, did she have to use it in front of everyone?"*

It never failed that there would be days when she seemed to have slipped into her own little world, and would sit on the stairs by J. Antonio Jarvis School - the elementary school near our house - and mumble to nobody in particular.

Those mean bullies would wait until I got off the school bus and torment me. They would laugh at me and gang up on me just calling me names like "Crazy Mary's daughter" or they would stupidly act as though mental illness was something you could catch, like a cold, and shun me like I was contagious. It also didn't help that my mother referred to me as "that child or that girl" on a regular basis. Those types of experiences at any age do something to you on the inside; but I was in elementary school, so it was very traumatic to say the least to feel like I would never fit in. I felt tormented and started to find solace internally.

Take it from me, that kind of torment causes you to retreat to a place in your mind where you are so strong that nothing and no one can bother you. Or so you think! What you don't realize is that each time an incident occurs, you retreat inside of yourself a little bit at a time, until one day you might not recognize who YOU are.

MY MATERNAL GRANDMA, DELIA SIMMONDS
AKA MAMA

CHAPTER TWO

Let's face it...My mom was crazy. There I admit it. But you know what? So are many other people. There's nothing for me to be ashamed of because it is just a part of the journey that is my life. Yes, she may have walked the streets of St. Thomas and cursed people out for no apparent reason, but she was still my mother. Her DNA flows through my body and helps to define who I am today. She had a family who loved her and tried to understand what had happened to her mind; what took her sanity away.

As her daughter, I prayed that this would never be my fate: that my children would not be ashamed to identify themselves as mine; or that they would never feel too embarrassed to hold their heads up when my name was mentioned. At least I can look in the mirror and embrace that part of my history because there are sure a lot of people running around here looking put together and cracking up on the inside. *Oops! Did I just say that out loud? I think "Self" might have just made her debut. Now where was I?* Oh, my point is that the adage about judging a book by its cover is true. There are lots of polished people or funny people posing as "happy" people, when in truth, they may be covering up a darker side of themselves that most people never see.

With my mother it was pretty gradual and quiet. It sort of sneaked up on all of us to be honest with you. She would display some pretty odd behaviors but because she didn't ever open up to anyone about what she was feeling or thinking, her parents didn't have a name for the changes they were seeing. I vividly recall one of the good days, when Mommy was taking me to school and singing "Baby don't worry, about a thing; 'cause every little thing's gonna be alright." You know, Bob Marley's famous song, "Three Little Birds." One of the other things that I recall is that she was rather overprotective of me and would walk me right to the door of my classroom in the mornings. She would also be the first parent waiting for the doors to open as the bell rang.

But sadly, those memories are few and far between, so I cherish them even more. But in spite of these happier moments there were definitely glimpses along the way that something was not right with her. We just couldn't put our finger on what it was at the time. You see, with my mother there were moments of lucidity and then there were times when she'd pull a disappearing act for days at a time. If the family was to be brutally honest, in my opinion, there were probably small signals that were missed because no one was paying close attention. My mother, as I said, was living on her own and was even a voting member of society; but then she started slacking off on her rent and simply refused to pay for the roof over her head. She also didn't talk much about things that were bothering her and could become almost like an ostrich, burying her head in the sand rather than face what was going on in her life. At some point during this time, Mama discovered that Mommy had become paranoid about germs and started taking baths in rubbing alcohol to keep her skin clean. These were all small signs that something was going on in her

14

brain, but we just didn't see it.

As a youngster, I lived with both sets of grandparents mixed in with time with my own parents. *No wonder I wound up having an outspoken, opinionated alter ego.* That's a lot of bouncing around for one person. Looking back, I guess I lost my innocence during this time because I was being exposed to life experiences that would cause me to grow up more quickly than my friends. I began to slowly notice changes in my mother's behavior and said so to my grandmother. For example, she began counting food. If she bought me a bunch of grapes, she would count every single grape. Then one random morning, mommy woke me up and accused me of eating one of her grapes. *Now mind you, in my head I was thinking, she's getting this worked up over ONE grape?* Little did I know that this was a telltale sign that would make sense down the road.

CHAPTER THREE

So what was it like growing up with a parent who was different? Well, I'm guessing that is how my opinionated, internal voice became so loud (*it's the part of my brain with no filter*). I did not have an easy childhood, period. If you think a cat has nine lives, then I must be one. In the early stages of my life I had a few incidents that could have taken me off this earth; but as I've heard constantly, I had angels watching over me. Just two days before my seventh birthday, I was hit by a car and suffered massive injuries. The truth is, I was pretty banged up; and given that I was mostly skin and bones at that age – or in more polite terms, petite – it's a wonder that I survived the accident at all.

It took six months for me to just learn how to walk again and unbeknownst to me, the long term prognosis was that I would not be able to have children. What I remember about that incident, though, is that my mother was crying, not just because she realized that she almost lost her only child, but also for the hard recovery ahead of me. During these moments in the hospital, I felt like every other child out there. And then, just like that, I was back to being in the "cuckoo's nest" again.

Two years later, my life was spared yet again. In the islands there aren't as many outside entertainment options for children as in the states, so one of the things we love to do is go swimming on the beach. During the summer of my 9th birthday, I was swimming at

Sapphire Beach on St. Thomas with my aunt (my dad's sister), her husband, and their two daughters. At some point I was playing out in the water by myself – keep in mind that I had no clue how to swim. There were sand dunes under the water so I thought the land was pretty level where I was. As I jumped and played in the water, it dawned on me that I was sinking so I began to yell and scream at the top of my lungs. However, there was no one around to help me. *All I kept thinking was why am I surrounded by all this water, and where the heck is everybody? In all honesty, it felt like my lungs, my nose and my eyeballs were rapidly filling up with water and my brain was slowly processing the fact that I was drowning – no kidding.* In what seemed like an instant I could swear that I was seeing that white light that you hear about when you are about to die, except that in my vision, there was a hand reaching for me then pulling back. Apparently I had passed out, so when I started to come to, I began throwing up and coughing uncontrollably.

I recall the nice paramedics telling me how lucky I was to be alive. What I later learned gave me chills though – I had stopped breathing for fifteen minutes but they would not give up on me. I guess one of my nine lives kicked in because it just was not my time to go. One glaring thing that was evident to me, however, was that my mother was not around during any of this. I thought it was strange, but I would later learn that no one could find her. She'd pulled one of her disappearing acts and by the time she turned up my grandparents didn't want to upset her.

Yes, my mom was very loving in her own way; but there was a time she tried to get me to smoke a joint and I burned my bottom lip because I was not sure what to do with it. My grandmother, her mother, was terribly upset because she felt that she was teaching me un-Godly habits like lying and keeping secrets at an early age. I remember being on my knees with her praying for forgiveness for I had sinned and wanted to repent so I wouldn't get in trouble with God. Later on that evening, my mother and grandma got into an argument over the example she was setting for me; luckily, my mother was coherent enough to realize that she was wrong and eventually apologized to both of us for what she had done. Mixed in with these occurrences were normal activities like play time with my second cousins who were my age. Since I was an only child, their mom, whom I call my Aunty Ruby, would invite Mommy and me to come over so I could bond with other children and have some fun. That's because my own first cousins were living on the U.S. mainland, so I didn't have a constant stream of playmates to interact with.

As simple as this gesture was, my mother had some sense of paranoia taking place in her mind, so although we were around family, she would remain outside of the house during my entire visit and not cross the threshold. Yet, she would never leave me there alone; nor would she even eat what was offered or use the rest room. *She just didn't seem to trust anyone with her child, but strangely enough she would allow me that little moment of normalcy, so what was really going on in her mind?* By the time I got to high school, she started spending more time outside of the house. She would go for hours, from sun up to sun down, sitting down on the waterfront on our beautiful island of St. Thomas, conversing with the water. This would go on for days and days.

As I mentioned, my community was pretty close knit; so people were always in our business. During my elementary school years, I took the bus from school to my grandmother's house, which happened to be down the street from the neighborhood elementary school. Most days in my sixth grade year, my last year in elementary school, my grandmother would meet me at the bus stop or I would walk with other children down the hill; but there were some days when my friend Janis or my cousins would come out to the bus stop and stick up for me with all those mean children taunting me about my mom. I became such an introvert because I didn't want to have to deal with the humiliation I felt on the inside.

You see, all this time, I felt maybe it was just all in my mind; that my mom was just different and as I progressed into my teenage years, the toll of my mother's illness began to really affect me. I started to encounter my own tendencies with depression, and felt that no one listened to me. From the summer before starting middle school, I spent most of my time with Mama, and the weekends, with my Uncle Sam. My mother was no longer working, and would spend a lot of her time by herself. She rarely took me anywhere with her, so I began to feel that I was the cause of whatever it was she was going through. Although my mother, my grandparents and I lived under one roof, it no longer felt like we were a family. She was no longer loving, no longer saying kind words, no longer singing. She just drifted...away into her own dark place where I could no longer reach or relate to her. It was during that time that I told Mama that I didn't want to return to school, but she put her foot down because she felt school was the best outlet for me to channel what was happening at home. *Don't get me wrong, I loved learning, but I did not like the torment that I received on a regular basis from those mean kids.* They had no regard for my feelings and probably never even considered how their words and actions made me feel on the inside. So, I developed this emotional barricade to give the appearance that I wasn't affected.

During the summer before I turned thirteen, my grandmother and my mom were having a heated conversation because my mother wanted to go somewhere and Mama thought it was not a good idea. I was somewhere in the living room while this was occurring and all of a sudden my mom glanced at me with a strange look before heading out of the door, which made the hair on the back of my neck stand up. It was really eerie and I was very afraid of what was going through her mind. I think my grandparents also sensed that Mommy had gone into a pretty scary place mentally because they were acting very overprotective and my grandmother was pacing and praying throughout the house. My grandmother and grandfather kept me away from the windows for the rest of the afternoon but I could tell that they were afraid about something totally unknown to me. It was like the calm before the storm.

CHAPTER FOUR

Out of nowhere, I heard arguing downstairs with my mom and my grandfather. Mommy came storming into the house and pulling me by my left arm through the front door with her. Instantly my grandmother was pulling on my right arm. I felt like a rope in a tug of war game, which my mother ultimately won by pulling on my hair. It was like a scene out of a movie. I am standing there between the two of them screaming each time she pulled my braid until she slapped me upside the head for yelling out. I felt frightened, confused, and hurt because this wasn't the mom I knew, who even in her weirdness let me know she loved me.

It was so totally out of character that I just got quiet. Things were happening so fast. Mom pulled me all the way up the hill by my braid and sat down at the bus stop to wait on the bus so we could go to wherever she was staying on the western end of the island. All I kept thinking was, *I don't have anywhere to sleep down there so where the hell is she taking me?* During this time, Mommy was talking to herself. Some of her words were clear but most of the time I had not a clue what she was uttering. I could just tell she was angry – at me!! I felt it coming through her pores but I didn't know for sure what I had done to set her off. For the next few moments, I reflected on the day's events: Mama's concern for me earlier that morning, the look on my mother's face before she left the house, my grandmother demanding that she not take me with her. I eventually came to the conclusion that it was a really bad idea for me to be in that apartment with my mother so I started plotting my escape to get back uptown to my grandmother's house. *This is a whole lot of drama for a soon to be thirteen year old to deal with, but hey, as they say, God knows best.*

When the bus finally came, I started putting my plan in motion to get off at the most opportune time. I recalled that the bus would stop at McDonald's so I decided to make my move by telling her that I needed to use the restroom. I really was praying that she would let me go alone but that didn't happen. I guess she didn't trust me because not only did she get off the bus with me; she came right into that bathroom with me and followed me into the stall. I don't know about you, but it's kind of hard to pee with someone staring at you, so nothing happened. This only led to me getting another slap in the head and being hurried to fix my clothes so we could leave. Mom grabbed me so forcefully that I was actually terrified that my mother was actually going to harm me. I felt in my spirit like I was going to die that day but something whispered to me that God was in control of what was taking place. What happened next would alter the course of my life – not just with my mother, but forever.

As we were exiting the restaurant, I kicked off my penny loafer shoe so that when we boarded the next bus, I had a reason to go back into McDonald's. By this time she was extremely pissed at me for delaying her plans so she threatened to beat the crap out of me when we got to her place – or as she said, when we got home. That place was NOT home for me, but I didn't dare express that out loud. She was so annoyed at me that she let go of my hand just long enough for me to get the hell off of that bus and make a run for it down the side walk. All I was hearing in my head was "Run Yas, run!" I ran down the street screaming for help; that my mother was going to hurt me and she was running right behind of me picking up speed. I recall seeing pedestrians trying to hold her back but she had this super strength and was just pushing them down like bowling pins. I don't know what had gotten into her that day but I knew I was in trouble. From behind I could hear her yelling, "Hold her, I am going to kill her!" *Wait just a second...Kill me? What did I do? I am the daughter she was supposed to protect and cherish. Now she's chasing me down the damn street like some crazed lunatic and I'm the problem?*

Now St. Thomas's waterfront is barely one mile long so this kind of madness is visible to every single person driving along the road. Some summer this was shaping up to be. I began crying as I ran, and all of a sudden I could no longer feel my legs touching the ground. It was like I was flying in the air. For a minute I wondered if God had sent his angels to protect me, and in a way he did. Just at that moment, a gentleman in the back of a painter's truck grabbed the back of my collar and pulled me up into the bed of the truck and drove me to their office suite so I could use the phone and call someone. I called my grandmother and my Uncle Sam and my "guardian angels" gave my mama directions to come and get me. Just as I was doing so, I heard this commotion outside and ran to the window to see what was going on. Just like in the movies, things were moving in slow motion. I watched in horror as my mother fought these men as they tried to calm her down. I remember pressing my face to the glass as the tears streamed down and just mumbling to myself for her to stop. It was too much. I had seen too much, experienced too much. I just wanted it to all go away. All I am thinking is how is this my life? What did I do to deserve this? Why is this happening to me? And how will I ever face anyone again?

Some moments later, three police cars pulled up followed by a man dressed in all white who was carrying a white cloth in his hands. The officers instructed the men to go inside but I was still standing there watching through the front glass. I wish now that they had taken me with them because I am forever traumatized, because the image of seeing my mother tackled to the ground by the officers with her face slammed into the street is burned into my memory for the rest of my life. They had placed her hands behind her back and forced her to stand. The man in all white, then walked up to her and placed this white cloth with zippers around the top portion of her body – almost like a life sized strip of gauze with zippers. I simply stared as they shoved her into this van and whisked her away. I think I was in shock. I didn't cry nor did I speak. I just stood there. Everything that happened next was a blur to me. I just shut down and became like a mannequin. I vaguely remember Mama repeating a prayer of protection over me and then in the days ahead we went to court for them to figure out what to do with me.

All of this happened during my twelfth year of life and it left an indelible mark on me that words cannot describe. I'm amazed that I didn't just go stark raving mad my damn self and check out altogether. It took everything I had within me to keep my pre-teen mind in the right place, but it was not easy. I started acting out and giving my grandmother a hard time because I felt rejected and unlovable. Since the Virgin Islands didn't have adequate facilities for mentally ill patients, my mother was only kept for a couple of days; however the damage had already been done. After witnessing all that craziness – pun intended – I became terrified of my mother. I honestly believe that my grandparents were afraid of her too, because they essentially slept with one eye open.

After that horrific incident, I locked myself in an emotional bubble where no one could get to me. Then, as if we hadn't been through enough, my grandfather Eric unexpectedly died from a heart attack and it felt like the walls were just crumbling all around us. All I could think was that I had lost everybody in one second and I was all alone. Yes, my grandmother was there but she is not the most touchy-feely individual, because she has had to be so strong for everyone else. I just didn't know how to deal with my own feelings and began to lash out and hating God. By my freshman year of high school I had basically shut down and refused to speak anymore. I mean, what was the point? My dad had basically done a disappearing act and my mother was stone cold out of her mind. Can you believe she would look me in the eye and just refer to me as 'that girl?' or 'that child?' I am her flesh and blood for crying out loud! I felt so rejected and abandoned, even though I had other family around me. My poor grandmother had no idea how to reach me and tried everything during that time to engage me on a daily basis. I had disconnected from my day to day, and was essentially failing the ninth grade.

CHAPTER FIVE

As if the personal trauma wasn't enough, I was still being ridiculed on a regular basis by the children at school. *I don't know about where you are from, but here in the islands, children were pretty tough on you if they didn't like you.* On the outside, they saw this pretty, quiet girl with long hair, but they had no idea what was eating me up on the inside. In my mind I saw a quiet girl whose grandmother made her wear long, "granny" or "grandma"-looking skirts to school when everyone else looked fashionable – or so I thought; the one with the crazy mother who didn't want to acknowledge her, but who followed her as she walked home from school, the one whose father was missing in action, with no interaction (and there wouldn't be much of that until I was well into adulthood). I often wondered what I had done to deserve this much dysfunction in my life but the answers never came, so I kept it all inside at the time. On top of that, I always acknowledged my mother, no matter what mental state she was in at the time, so the kids at school knew that my family life was not like everyone else's. In today's terms it felt like I was living out a reality show where all eyes are on you.

At her wits end, especially after Grandfather Eric's death, my grandmother tried everything she could to bond with me during that time. As I mentioned, Granny believed in tough love, and she made it clear that she would not be cuddling me as I went through my dark period. At first she tried to encourage me to learn to cook…no response; then she suggested gardening…again, no response. Finally, one day when she was sewing, a light came on in my eyes and Mama realized that she had found something that could hold my interest and bring me out of my emotional coma. She herself was a great seamstress, and she would make the skirts for my school uniform. *Yes, in the Virgin Islands and throughout many Caribbean islands, school students wear uniforms with pleated skirts to school as a way to instill discipline in the students. But I digress...*the challenge was that while my grandmother sewed so well, her idea of a school skirt was one that came all the way down to my shins. Needless to say that in the late 80s this was absolutely not the fashion trend that a child wanted to have, much less at the high school level. I mean, I was already being teased for so much else, why add my wardrobe to the mix, right? Essentially, once my brain wrapped itself around the art of sewing, it was a new day for me. I recall my grandmother making me a skirt for our choir concert and I badgered her to make it much shorter, like up to my knees. *Could I just get a little slack please?* Well, the argument that ensued resulted in my Mama telling me, "Fine, make it yourself;" and I, with my fast mouth said, "Fine, then show me," and the rest as they say is history.

In that moment, Mama realized that she had found something that made me come alive, so she provided instruction on how to sew the pleats and put on the waistband, then gave me the creative freedom to design my own version of the skirt. With a new-found focus on sewing, it became a lifeline that pulled me out of a very, very dark and depressed place. I was allowed to spend more time on the sewing machine but only after I had done my homework. Given that I had "checked out" for almost an entire school year, this was major progress and I found a healthy way to express myself and bring my own identity to the forefront. By the end of the school year, those same children who had tortured me or just flat out ignored me, began to take notice of the skirts I was wearing to school. After all those years – from elementary school to high school - the bullying that had sapped my spirit was over, at least for now. I had finally found acceptance, and believe it or not, I wound up designing and sewing their school skirts for them – for a fee, of course! *Now isn't that something?*

JOURNEY UNTOLD: TWISTED LOVE –
MY MOTHER'S STRUGGLE WITH MENTAL ILLNESS

CHAPTER SIX

Not having my mother around in a parental role did have an impact on my life, but I don't think I truly grasped that until much later in life. Although things calmed down a bit at school, the turmoil in my life was far from over. I would see her along the street, usually following behind me as I walked home from school. Though she would not speak directly to me, or acknowledge me, it was as if she wanted to keep an eye on me. I, on the other hand, was rather embarrassed and nervous at the same time, because I was never sure what her reaction or response would be when I encountered her. This of course made it difficult to fit in and have any semblance of a normal existence throughout my teenage years. As a result, I didn't have much of a social life in high school. Most people thought I was crazy too, so that stigma did not do much for me in the boyfriend department. Folks were also afraid of my mother and since they didn't know how she would react to them being around me, they just kept their distance. That was the case for most people, but not the two young ladies who would become my best friends in the world, even today.

My girls, Janis and Simone, were my safe place in the midst of the madness and they have a special place in my heart. During a time when I lived life in a fog, they were my foundation and stuck up for me many times when no one else would. Back then I felt marked for life as the crazy woman's child, like I was being punished for something I had done wrong. I also felt damaged and ugly, on the inside and out because it seemed like I was unlovable. Every day I would ask God to give me my mother back so that my life could be 'normal' again. What I didn't understand at the time was that this was the life that I had been given and it would be up to me to make the very best of it. After a very tumultuous start, my sophomore and junior years turned out to be fairly low key. Then, during the summer before starting my senior year, things changed. I was hanging out with my older cousin and her boyfriend one afternoon, and waiting for them to get ready so we could go out. The boyfriend also had one of his buddies at her house with him, so it was the four of us. As we were waiting, I remember thinking that they were taking awfully long to come outside – boy was I naive. At any rate, the "buddy" suggested that we go for a drive since they were still occupied.

Not knowing any better, I said sure. The next thing I know I am somewhere far from town, on the other side of the island in this dude's car. Fully alert now, I am eerily aware that I have no idea where I am because I was not yet driving, and I didn't tell anyone where I was going. Hell, I didn't even know this guy's real name, just the nickname I heard my cousin's boyfriend calling him. In a split second, the atmosphere changed and this fool was trying to take my innocence away from me. Somewhere deep in his mind I had been coming on to him, and had given him the green light. All I could think of was that I had to get out of there and I had to fight. So I fought and I fought, scratching and kicking until it was over. It was like time had stopped and I felt myself closing into a shell. In and in all honesty, I don't remember how long it was before I got home. I knew that something terrible had happened but I didn't have the heart to tell anyone. I just couldn't, I mean who was going to believe that I didn't bring this upon myself? I just wanted to get home, take a shower, crawl under the covers, and forget that this day had ever happened. Remember, I had never had a boyfriend and as you can imagine, my grandmother was not going to sit down and explain the birds and the bees to me, but I can assure you that this was not how it was supposed to happen.

What happened in the car is more complicated than I can share, but suffice it to say it was a life altering moment. By the time my senior year rolled around, I was sixteen, pregnant, and wondering what would become of my life now. Just when things were starting to go so well and people were beginning to accept the real me. I knew from the beginning that I was not going to have an abortion. That just goes against everything I believe in, but I also felt as though God was giving me a chance to lose the stigma that mental illness had placed over my life. Looking back now, I believe that this baby was a gift, but at the time, I and my pregnant state were a source of embarrassment and disappointment for my family – especially my father's side. After I decided to embrace motherhood, I put my focus on finishing school and raising my baby. With unwavering support from Mama, I was able to plan ahead for my future. I was fortunate to have been granted a part-time position in the Corporation Division of the Office of the Lieutenant Governor, which enabled me to hone my professional and technical skills in the workforce.

My immediate supervisor was a wonderful woman who admired my desire to work hard and my ability to utilize the computer systems her office had just installed to organize their documents in a digital format. Sometimes things happen in a way that only God can design. It turned out that my supervisor had a relative who suffered from mental illness so she totally understood my plight. Finally, I had found someone with whom I could honestly and openly sit, shake my head, and find humor in my mother's situation. She was the only other person at the time that I had ever met with a relative who had the same condition, and it felt good not to be judged, but accepted. *I finally felt like I was not alone!* Throughout the course of my after school employment, my supervisor and I developed a connection that would later open doors for me.

In June 1988, I crossed the stage with my high school diploma in hand and a desire to make something of my life. I was hired on full-time at my job and was finally feeling like things were coming together. Our offices sat on Government Hill – the area on St. Thomas where the Governor's and Lieutenant Governor's administrative offices are located – adjacent to each other. One day while we were working, I heard a woman yelling from down in the street, "Where is my husband, the Governor?" This was followed by a long, loud cackling as she laughed to herself while walking up the hill. Now keep in mind that I said I worked on the third floor; well guess whose office was below us on the second floor? My boss, the Lieutenant Governor, with the same open windows that were in our office! Whenever this happened – *yes, there was more than one incident –*

my supervisor would call me into her office so that we could yell back at her to be quiet, and she would just wave at us. *Oh my goodness. How could this woman come up here to my job and embarrass me like this? I just wanted to fall into the floor and disappear. What if everyone can hear her?* One day, the Lieutenant Governor called me downstairs into his office and asked me if the lady who yelled from down in the street was my mother. I remember standing there shaking, willing myself not to pee at that very moment. *After all, this was only the second highest ranking official in our homeland waiting for my response, but hey, no pressure!* I held my head down in shame, praying that I wasn't about to be fired, apologized for her behavior, and said yes to answer his question. *In the back of my mind I was thinking...great, now something good is going to be taken away yet again because of her. First my childhood, now THIS?! Was I ever going to be free of this worthless feeling? Geez!*

As a side note, I know you're probably thinking, how I could be so informal with the Lieutenant Governor. However in a small community like ours, with about 50,000 people on an island, you often know your elected officials on a personal level, or run into them in the stores as they shop. Oftentimes the officials are pretty down to earth so it's not difficult to speak to them as "regular" people. Minutes seemed to pass, but in reality it was probably just a few seconds. The Lieutenant Governor stood up and told me in a very calming and funny manner that he just wanted to meet the young lady that he had heard nothing but good things about and to put a face to the name. After that day, it became like a joke between him and me whenever my mom would pass by asking to see her husband. *What a relief. Thank God he didn't react differently. Maybe there was hope that I could live my own life after all.* I would learn decades later from my good friend Juel that my mother not only called out, but actually went up to the Governor's office to bring him toiletries from his "wife."

OMG, she brought the Governor of the United States Virgin Islands toilet paper, toothpaste, and a toothbrush? Lord, Jesus, take me now! The Governor seemed to know that she would bring these things to him and allowed her to leave them with the staff and confirm that he received them, just to appease her. *Talk about pleasing your constituents. Remember, my mother was registered to vote now, but even if she didn't vote, as a resident she was entitled to go and see her elected leader. Only my mother…good grief. I wonder what his REAL wife thought?!*

CHAPTER SEVEN

One day I was feeling a bit overwhelmed at work and decided to take a stroll through our downtown park, called Emancipation Garden. I saw a man giving modelling lessons and given that I sewed all my own clothing, my interest was immediately piqued. The gentleman, Mr. Lee, was an older male with an American (or as we say stateside) accent and when we started to speak about what he was doing, he asked me if I wanted to model. *Me? He wanted this shy, quiet chick to model clothing in front of people? Uh, uh.* But…somewhere deep inside I really wanted to do it. Right there on the spot Mr. Lee took my hand and began to walk me through the fundamentals of modeling. I returned to the office feeling refreshed and excited about the possibilities that lay ahead. I returned to Mr. Lee's modeling school and quickly learned the ropes. Thanks to my Uncle Sam's assistance, I had been able to purchase a little red Volkswagen Fox, which came in handy with all the back and forth I had to do to manage my job, my son, and my newfound modeling career. It felt like the stars were lining up in my favor, or on a spiritual note, that God had finally started to smile on me. *But how could He, when I was steadily questioning whether or not He was really in my corner?* Modeling allowed me to feel beautiful and sexy – at least on the outside, and be accepted for the garments I wore. *If I could be appreciated for my outer beauty then no one would discover the misery and pain that was eating away at me on the inside. Right?*

During this summer I met my first boyfriend Leroy. Believe it or not, this was the first time in my life I had opened myself up enough to another person to let them in; and it was the first time I allowed myself to fall in love. It's actually kind of funny how we met. I was at a dance with my friend Simone and he dropped the corniest line on me saying, "You look so sweet you look like syrup." Well, the look I gave him was anything but sweet or syrupy and it was followed by a good old Caribbean suck teeth. *I mean how lame is that? Come on, dude!* Simone and I just walked away laughing, while he kept referring to me as "Syrup." A few days later, she called me to say that the 'syrup dude' showed up at her job looking for me. *First of all, how the heck did he know where she worked? Can you say stalker? But, in truth, that showed a little creativity on his part, and he was kind of cute. Aww hell...I actually fell for his goofy antics.*

Around the same time, I was making plans to go to college. I knew from day one that I was not going to be a statistical teenage mother; I was going to college. Period. Once my mind was made up, Mama and Uncle Sam pitched in to help me so I could start college in August of 1989. My uncle would help to support my studies and my grandmother would keep my son until I got settled in at school. In my heart I wanted to be a fashion designer. I had expressed this to my uncle a couple years earlier, but he plainly told me he wasn't paying for me to go to college for that, and sent me to the library *(yes people, this was LONG before Google)* to look up good paying jobs. My research back then didn't turn up any Virgin Islands-born fashion designers, but I have since learned that there are a few out there. *Uncle Sam seems to have no recollection of this chain of events, but we do get a good laugh out of it now.*

After relaying my findings, I told my uncle that I would attend college to study business with a minor in travel and tourism. Unbeknownst to him, I was still creating a vision in my mind that I would be known for my designs and that my clothing would be featured on the red carpet. As the time neared for me to leave for school in Florida, it became incredibly difficult and heart-wrenching to leave my nine-month old son behind. While in my head I knew that this was a necessary move to create a better life for the two of us, in my heart I was terrified. *After all, I did not want him to feel abandoned in any way, and trust me, children do know these things regardless of their ages.* The reality was that I needed more than a high school diploma to fulfill my dreams and to be able to take care of both of us. I said my goodbyes and promised him that I would come back to visit on every break *(thankfully there are direct flights between Ft. Lauderdale and St. Thomas that are just a couple of hours).*

This was the start of a two-year journey that would be a game-changer for my son and me, and I cried from lift off to landing, not knowing what the future held for us. I settled into my new place and threw myself into student mode. On the first day of class, I met a young lady from the Bahamas who would become my roommate for those two long years. Interestingly enough, she was majoring in

Fashion Design! Go figure. *Yes, I happened to conveniently pick a technical college that offered majors in travel & tourism and fashion design. That was just my determined mind at work.* I taught her about business and she taught me about fashion design. During my last semester, I went to the school's dean, showed him my good grades, and asked him if I he would allow me to take three design classes required to graduate with an additional degree in fashion design. I was motivated by the desire to provide my son with the best life possible so I shared with the dean how I had consistently been on the Dean's list, even after I went back to St. Thomas to get my son so he could be with me. The dean learned that other students in the dorms would help me by babysitting between classes and he, too, was amazed by my determination. He then agreed that if I took the classes at night he would authorize the dual degree track for me, so that is exactly what I did for the last six months of school, with my toddler in tow. By that time, I had also taken on a position as manager of a retail store to ensure that I could pay for my new classes, because my uncle's words were still ringing in my ears. Although I was super excited that I was studying the fashion industry, I didn't feel that I could be completely honest with any of my relatives – especially Uncle Sam. *I could not muster the courage to possibly tell my family that I was going to have a career in fashion despite their warnings. I decided to just send them a graduation announcement and say, 'By the way, I am graduating with a dual degree in business and fashion design.'* Nonetheless, as if I didn't have enough on my plate, I decided to audition for an MTV fashion show at my school. I made it through to the final rounds and was selected to participate, making this my first runway modeling gig in the United States. It felt so good to be forming my own identity without judgment because of my mother. I was beginning to relish my independence, which became even more important once my first love and I ended our relationship. *The long distance had just become too much for the both of us, but we have remained friends to this day.* For the first time in a very long time I felt normal; and it felt fantastic.

I graduated from college with my two degrees in hand and my little son in the cheering section – I don't think I invited anyone else to attend my ceremony. I returned to St. Thomas and started working in the local Chase Bank and it almost felt like I had never left. Immediately I began to miss the anonymity that comes with living away and I started to retreat inward again. To shake of the insecurity and self-consciousness, I went back to modeling with Mr. Lee so that it appeared from the outside that I was still confident. *Even I knew that I was fooling myself, but hey, you have to fake it 'til you make it sometimes.* No sooner than I started all of this, my mother was strolling up and down the Charlotte Amalie waterfront all day, and my workplace was right in the middle of that stroll. Later that year, I met the man who would become the father of my second son. This man was so smooth and had apparently been checking me out from afar. One day I was on the beach and my ex-boyfriend and I were having a brief conversation. After I went about my business, this man walked right up to him and asked him who I was. A few days later he even had his best friend call me up to tell me how much he cared about me. *Do people still do that after age 14? I have to say he was rather persistent, which*

45

should have been a red flag for me to pay attention to his behavior, but you know how it is when you are swept off your feet. Since I was pretty introverted when off stage, I typically did not socialize with others, because I suspected they were gossiping about me behind my back. I remember thinking, *"This fine man must be crazy to be talking to me, doesn't he know I have a mother who really is crazy? ... and did he just sit down on the beach to play with my son and me? I guess people would just have to talk."*

It would be close to a year before I let the new guy come close to my heart strings, but that did not deter him. He continued to persist and pursue me. I asked myself if I could honestly let another person in and trust them with my love? *In hindsight, I realize that all of the abandonment issues and devastation surrounding my mother's illness were keeping me from giving and receiving love.* When I finally let my guard down, I gave him 100 percent of me and loved him from his toe nails to his soul. I just loved all of him. During this time, I switched jobs and transitioned from banking to working in travel and tourism for a company that advertised the port lectures on board the cruise ships. I felt so at home that I began to come alive once again. My employers were so cool. Though they were from the Virgin Islands, they rarely got caught up in the local drama and they had no clue who my mother was. *Nada.* They just knew that I was a good employee who loved her job and them because I was good at masking my real feelings about everything.

As my relationship progressed, I pushed aside my hesitations and decided to go full force with my heart leading the way. Our relationship was still new but we decided to move in together and start our life. Within a few months of living together I found out that I was pregnant and needless to say it came as quite a surprise. It wasn't that long ago that my doctor had told me that there was a very high probability that I would not ever have children again because of a blockage in my fallopian tubes. I would subsequently undergo a series of surgeries to increase my chances of conception but for it to happen so quickly? I did not see that coming. *Besides, Mama had already warned me that she wasn't taking in another child to raise. What was I going to do?* In the fifth year of our relationship, my boyfriend started to show a completely different side of himself. I went from being his girlfriend to his possession. After going through a lifetime of feeling like my mother's possession, I certainly was NOT willing to become another person's object. I began to speak up for myself, which led to verbal, and later, physical abuse. The last straw came when he put a knife to my throat. By then, I was completely stripped of my self-esteem and had lost all interest in sewing; and that's saying a lot. Like most victims of abuse, I was too embarrassed to tell my family or seek help. *I mean, how could I tell them that I had screwed up yet again by choosing a less than favorable partner?* I just knew in my spirit that I had to get out of the situation on my own, so I packed up my things and left St. Thomas for good. I have since only returned to visit, and do so frequently, but I just could not take being stained yet again with the stigma of one more bad thing in my life. I had just had enough!

My departure would turn out to be a blessing in disguise as this was 1994 and one of the most ferocious hurricanes the islands would ever see would hit the island one year later. With my hasty departure, I pretty much hit the reset button on life and seemingly dropped off the face of the earth. I even lost contact with my childhood friends Simone and Janis. *If it wasn't family, I really wasn't trying to make contact. It was just something that I needed to do to make it through that leg of my journey.* When I left St. Thomas, I realized that I couldn't manage with my oldest son and an infant, so I made the ridiculously painful decision to leave my eldest with my grandmother for a little while. There are no words to describe what it felt like to have to make that choice. I felt like I had a hole in my soul, and more than anything I didn't want him to feel abandoned yet again, especially now that he was older and a little more aware. As parents we often make decisions in the moment that are the best we can do at that time – and this thought has given me a little more insight into why my mother may have initially made arrangements for my godparents to raise me when I was born.

As I relocated to Florida with my little one, I replayed the past year in my mind and had to ask myself what it was about me that there was so much dysfunction in my life. Keep in mind, I was only in my mid-twenties but so much had happened that I felt as though I had lived a thousand lifetimes already. I made a vow to God that I was never going to love again because in MY world, love equaled pain. *I know this may sound rather cynical, but let's face it, my track record in matters of the heart was not looking so great – my mother and father seemed to want nothing to do with me, my first child was conceived in an unloving way, and the second man I gave my heart to used his love to beat my spirit out of me. I was surely batting a big, fat zero.* With just $2000 to my name, and no source of employment, I made up my mind to rely on myself. I developed a special friendship with a young lady who gave us shelter during my transition because she respected and admired my drive to make things right for myself. It turns out that I knew her then-boyfriend, now husband, but she and I had never met until arrived in Miami. Her generosity paved the way for us to become very good friends but even with all she had done to help me I was guarded. During that time, my Uncle Sam also saw the positive changes in me since I left the island and offered to assist me in purchasing my first home. *Finally, a sense of normalcy and stability. Perhaps now I could have a life with a little less drama. Lord, who was I kidding?*

As part of my fresh start, I went back to school to become certified in computer science I had an interest in computers and it was a field in which I could grow. I had a new life and a new career, helping others learn how to navigate this new computer era. Around 1997, things were looking up and I climbed the ladder rapidly in my company, and then later at another firm. It was during this move that I met my now ex-husband. What caught my attention with him was how differently he treated me. He had a huge heart and took care of everything for me, including helping me in my career, but most importantly he treasured me. He was everything that everyone else who claimed to love me was not. Unfortunately, this is what attracted me to him, so I loved him for all the wrong reasons. Looking back now, I know that I was wrong to let him think the feelings were mutual. *Believe me, it wasn't that I didn't care for him; I did. I just didn't know how to love someone without it causing me tremendous pain.* After everything I'd been through up to that point in my life I had created an emotional bubble around myself to avoid feeling anything and everything. I had even convinced myself that I was this brand new person; that I had reinvented myself. I threw myself into my modeling career and bought into my own hype that I was as happy as I looked in the photographs. I essentially created a whole new scenario without sharing any major details about my past trauma or my dysfunctional upbringing with the new man in my life.

I was setting the stage for failure and didn't even see it coming, but as they say, what's done in the dark must come to light; and it did. I had been in Florida about three or four years before meeting my ex-husband and as things progressed, I became pregnant with my third child, my son Riki, who was born autistic. It was a very difficult pregnancy and delivery, so much so that I was told that trying to give birth another time could cost me my life! This was like a death sentence to me because I so desperately wanted to try for a little girl. It was almost like an obsession for me, to the point where if I went into a store and passed the girls' clothing, I would have a major meltdown. I loved my children, my boys, but all I wanted was the chance to become the mother that mine could not be, and try to build upon her legacy by raising a little girl into a strong, dynamic woman. Looking back now, I was still doing so with my sons, but at the time it just didn't feel like enough.

One day, I was in a store, and was so overcome by emotion that I literally fell out on the floor crying hysterically because I felt robbed of the gift of having a girl child. *So maybe I was losing it just a tad. What in the world was I being so melodramatic about when God had blessed me with my beautiful boys?* After talking with my husband about my desires, we made the decision to adopt our daughter. We initially tried to do so in the U.S., but there were so many rules and restrictions, particularly if you wanted to adopt a child from another racial background. After months of research, we settled on Cambodia, a country where they were happy for couples to adopt their orphaned children, so we worked with an agent who helped to make our dream a reality.

On March 19, 2001, we began our quest with the adoption process to bring our daughter home, and on May 19, 2001, we received our referral photo of her from the agent. It was then we learned that she had been born on the day we began the adoption. *I think this was God's way of telling us she was the daughter he created just for us.* Her birth name was Rath Chouck Chan. Rath means orphan in Cambodian, but my husband and I decided to blend our family names to give her the name Yamisha. On August 17, 2001, my husband and I boarded a plane for Cambodia to meet Yamisha for the first time. It was a rather long plane ride to the other side of the world, and we arrived two days later on August 19, 2001, five months after our little girl had been born.

Despite this happy occasion, the core of my marriage had been shaken several months before when I first took my husband to St.

Thomas to meet my family and to inform them about our decision to adopt. During the course of the visit, after five years of secrecy and half-truths, I decided to disclose the truth about my past and my family history. *Let's just say that he was <u>not</u> happy, and I can't say that I blamed him.* He was shocked and more than a little bit upset, and told me that I had built a life for us that was based on a complete lie. Once again, I had allowed my mother's madness to have control over the choices I made. In hindsight, I was wrong to have done that to him, and I now realize that you have to own up to everything you are in order to love and accept the reflection in the mirror. It became evident that my true reason for not being able to love him fully was because I didn't love myself, but after disclosing my truth, it opened the door for me to begin my journey to healing myself.

CHAPTER EIGHT

With Yamisha, or Misha as we call her, in our lives, I felt like a missing piece of the puzzle of my life had fallen into place. For the first time since my abusive relationship, I found my passion for sewing again, and I followed my intuition and took a chance to create custom clothing for small children. I had found my happy place again and uncovered a new skill of designing patterns and outfits without any prior experience. I called the line Yammiwear and established Yammi Boutique in honor of our daughter. Things were going pretty well for us, but when my daughter turned two years old, I noticed signs of her retreating inward, which could have been a result of the instability and transition that comes with being a foster child. Our daughter was a beautiful and photogenic toddler and though there were offers, we were careful not to throw her into the world of modeling if it wasn't something she was comfortable with.

In time, though, we decided to let her build her confidence through beauty pageants, and it turned out that we had found the thing that made her come alive. Yamisha's confidence continually improved and she blossomed each time she hit the stage. It was in these competitions that she first spoke in public and began to perform with ease. This was 2005, and during this time, my older children entered me into a local pageant – the adult version of the Our Little Miss (OLM) Beauty pageant in which I had entered my daughter Yamisha - without my knowledge, while they were at the mall. My eldest son, Roumell, talked the other two into it because he recalled me having a dream of competing in the Miss Virgin Islands pageant. Roumell felt that had it not been for my getting pregnant with him as a teenager that I could have fulfilled that dream, and he wanted me to know what it felt like to compete. He must have overheard me talking one day and took it as a personal quest to help me achieve this. What he didn't know was that I had also competed in and won the Miss Caribbean Tourism (1996) during my younger days. What my son also didn't realize was that he was a blessing to me, so there were no regrets where he was concerned. It was just touching that as young as he was, he wanted to make my dreams come true. *I get teary-eyed just thinking about it, especially now that I don't see that side of him anymore.*

Nevertheless, I went along with it and won the darn thing! What a surprise to all of us, especially since it meant that I would have to compete at the state level for this competition, the Mrs. Florida State OLM Beauty Pageant. The night of the pageant, I gave it all I had, and when they announced yours truly as the winner of the state pageant it was total pandemonium. You should have seen us, my husband, the four children, all jumping up and down with excitement, and me, like a deer in headlights thinking *what on Earth have I gotten myself into?* I was absolutely terrified. Why? *Because I was old – over thirty and a mother...HELLO?!* But, here I was, doing something that I thought I would never achieve, thanks to my kids and the support of my husband. So as I am here racking up these crowns and titles, I was starting to see myself in a positive light, and realizing just what the pageants must have been doing for Yamisha on a positive level as well. In fact, we became the first mother-daughter duo to compete and hold titles at the same time. After capturing the state title, I realized that I would have to step my game up to compete in and win the Mrs. World OLM Beauty Pageant in Texas later that year. So, I hired a pageant coach to increase my chances for success. Since this competition was out of state, my family couldn't travel with me, but I had a good support group of moms from my daughter's pageants so I was in great hands.

Honestly, I still could not believe that I was doing this. After all, I was a small island girl with a tarnished image. How could I compete with all these beautiful women who seemed to have it all together? When the time came for the interview questions, I made up my mind then that I was going to be my authentic self and not paint a pretty picture of who I was. The judges asked me to explain what type of role model I was for my daughter as a mother competing in the pageant. I needed to be real and peel back the layers to unveil my true self so that I could be a positive example for all of my children. I don't know what came over me in that moment, but I actually admitted that my mother was mentally ill, and proceeded to explain to them (in a closed room) just how much my past had impacted me to strive for a much better parenting experience of my own. I was so engrossed in my response that I didn't even notice that the judges were all in tears with their pens down on the table, completely mesmerized. All I knew in that moment was that I felt free. In fact, I no longer cared if I won or lost. To quote Oprah, that was an 'AHA!' moment for me, a pivotal turning point in me choosing to unburden myself from my mother's twisted love and to choose a life of happiness and authenticity.

When the time came for the finalists to be announced, I placed in the top five. I was so full of joy for that outcome that I didn't even hear them call me as the winner. Quite frankly, I was still in shock that I had opened up so candidly in the interview room, and I wasn't condemned for my truth. I could not believe that I had won by opening up and being completely honest. I would later go on to compete and win the title of America's Fabulous Faces Queen later that year. This was yet another turning point on my journey; one that would provide me with the strength I needed for the things to come. As I went through my year as Mrs. World OLM Beauty, things were shattering at home. I became very proficient at hiding my pain behind my smile but it was hurting my marriage. All the lies I had told to cover up who I really was and other incidents that had taken place had just become too much to bear. I made the decision to leave and really focus on what was best for me. My husband was hurt and probably viewed me as a selfish woman for choosing myself and my sanity over a life with him, but it was for the best. I needed to learn how to love myself and make peace with the woman in the mirror. *Yes, I am channeling Michael Jackson right about now… [singing] "I'm starting with the [woman] in the mirror, woo hoo. I'm asking [her] to make a change…"*

Let me just say this – there is nothing like a divorce for you to really see the other side of the person you are married to. In the end, it was a very angry and spiteful divorce that left us both feeling battered and bruised, because he wouldn't let me go and I was determined not to stay. This was especially difficult on the children. They were confused, hurt, and divided. My family was split apart, and I had once again lost my passion for sewing, just as I was putting the pieces of my life together. I had to struggle not to feel like a victim for once, but everything was in disarray. It would be five long and painful years before my marriage could be officially dissolved, and in 2009, the divorce was finally completed.

A few months later, my phone rang, and in the blink of an eye, things would never be the same. My oldest son, Roumell had been shot and was fighting for his life. All I could think was where did I go wrong and what would happen to him now? What would I do if he didn't make it, and how would I share this news with the other kids? It was such a blur, and after all my previous years of cursing God for not protecting me, I started to see that there really were angels here on Earth. In one instance after the other there were little miracles that took place in order for my son to be alive today, and for that I am eternally grateful. My faith in God was renewed by the events that occurred to save Roumell's life and once he was out of the danger, my passion for sewing was restored; however, this time I began to focus on women's clothing. In the midst of my crisis, I owned up to my wrongs and the way I treated, or mistreated, my ex-husband. It was the beginning of a journey of forgiveness, one that has allowed us to be better parents to the children. But there was more bad news on its way. I just didn't know that God had been preparing me for this blow all along.

CHAPTER NINE

On June 6, 2009, I received a phone call that would soon alter my world, yet again. My grandmother called to tell me that my mother had been hospitalized but she did not indicate that anything was time sensitive or critical. When she got around to telling me what was happening, I learned that my mother had been diagnosed with Stage 4 breast cancer. As Mama recounted the details, all I could think was I was about to lose my mother again, and this time for good. You see, by this time Mommy had been coming and going between my grandmother's house and the streets. She would leave for most of the day then return home in the evenings, but she was basically home. My mother was receiving food stamps and my grandmother would shop for her so that she had adequate food to eat. One day, my grandmother noticed that she had not been out for quite some time and went to check on her. Each time she did so, my mother would say she was resting and did not feel like going out, but she would usually come upstairs to the main part of the house to eat. This went on for about one month until my grandmother noticed a strange odor whenever my mom was nearby. Mama thought it was because she wasn't bathing on a regular basis and told her so, but my mom just stared blankly at her.

During one of the shopping trips, my mother went along and my grandmother noticed that Mommy didn't have the strength to walk alongside her. Keep in mind that this was a woman who walked miles every day just because, so not being able to keep up with an eightysomething-year-old woman was cause for speculation. As a matter of fact, she was sitting every chance that she got, so Mama told my mom that she was taking her to the emergency room. My mother refused; more than once. Since the odor and the fatigue persisted, my grandmother continued to insist that Mommy see a doctor, and each time she would refuse. Not sure what else to do, my grandmother called my mom's mental health counselor to have her committed out of concern for her overall health. She didn't like the way my mother looked or the lack of energy she had and she had begun to fear that my mother was very sick.

Ultimately, my mother told my grandmother that she would not seek medical attention unless forced to do so by the courts, so Mama had to get a court order to have my mother admitted to the hospital for a check-up. Well, when that day finally came, the police showed up at the front door to escort them to the hospital. They, too, smelled this foul odor and questioned where it was coming from, but no one could figure it out. When they got my mother to the hospital, she went through the admission process and was assigned a nurse. As she was undressing to have a bath, the nurse let out a blood curdling scream. As everyone came running, it became apparent why the odor was so strong – both of my mother's breasts were rotting away and she was completely oblivious to it. As nauseating as this thought is, it appears that my mother didn't even know she should be in pain. Her primary comment to the hospital staff was to ask why they were keeping her there and then say she was going home. Because she refused treatment, the attending staff had to give her a sedative so that they could ascertain the severity of her condition, something that even she didn't understand. After my mother was evaluated, she was admitted to the hospital for treatment. It was during her two week stay there, that my mother's mind came back long enough for her to realize that she was really sick.

The severity of her condition became even clearer, after the doctor explained that her cancer was in an advanced stage, and it would be necessary for her to start having chemotherapy at the Cancer Treatment Center. However, despite the doctor's explanation, my mother decided that she did not want the treatment, and declared that no one was putting that kind of poison in her body. Once again, my grandmother had to go to court, after speaking with the psychiatrist, to get my mother the treatment she needed. The courts gave my grandmother the legal authority to get the treatment going, but it still took some convincing to get Mommy to say yes. Bear in mind, it had been two to three weeks with no treatment for breast cancer. It wasn't until the courts gave my grandmother legal custody of my mother, that she finally agreed to treatment. I flew down to St. Thomas to see her towards the end of her battle with the cancer and in a rare moment of lucidity my mother looked me in the eye and called me by my actual name. After thirty-plus years of longing to hear her speak to me with the love of someone who gave birth to me, it was on her death bed that she finally set me free. Then, just like that she was back in her mental shell, but I felt a sense of peace wash over me that would carry me through the days ahead.

At her funeral I was able to say goodbye by writing my thoughts in a farewell letter to my mother:

A LETTER TO MY MOM by Yassin Sirri Hall
(reprinted in its entirety)

For the 12 years that I have truly known you as my mom, you were the most beautiful, smart, loving, spiritual, funniest and the silliest mom I know. I remember so much, our spiritual Bob Marley nights and our times just sitting on the waterfront singing. I even remember the very first movie you took me to. The Harder They Come – Jimmy Cliff Movie. These are the times I will treasure for the rest of my life.

You made me who I am today and I am proud to say that I am your daughter. I have NEVER been ashamed of this.

I was told that when I was born you were so happy, you wanted to find the most perfect name for me. I remember in my room you had the words peaceful and loving all over it, the meaning of my name as I was told by you.

I remembered as a child I really hated my name LOL. When asked my name I always got, oh that's different or what did you say...I remember thinking Gosh can I just be normal LOL.

Now as an adult I LOVE my name, it symbolizes my uniqueness, my being, my individuality, my belonging, my destiny, my inner and outer self, it IS who I am. I am proud to say my mom gave me that name and I thank you.

As I young child, I wondered why you weren't like the other moms, but gently tossed the question out my mind because I too was not like the other kids. I never cried, I always laughed regardless of the situation. It was easier for me to laugh than to cry. I just knew you as my mom.

I remember the times you sat with me on the waterfront and we laughed and laughed at nonsense [LOL] but my biggest memory is when you would sing Three Little Bird's by Bob Marley and I would sing along. As I sit here and write this I am listening to the words imagining you singing it to me as the tears pour down my face.

After losing you mentally, I could never listen to the song ever until 2008 on your birthday. I played it over and over again and cried and cried. I feel it was when I became a true woman and that was my moment.

I remember every time you sang this part "cause every little thing gonna be all right!" you would touch my nose and smile at me. It was OUR MOMENT A MOMENT I WILL TREASURE FOREVER.

Though not all moments I would like to remember BIG SIGH AND LAUGHTER!!!! Through all my life's most embarrassing moments I still didn't quiver or cry. Because of you no matter what has been said or done it could never be worse than those embarrassing moments I have had with you.

Thank you for those moments as well (big sarcasm) ROTFL

Throughout life people would say to me "what ever happened to your mom? well please just don't let IT happen to you! Or hope you don't end up like your mother.

For years this is the only thing that ever bothered me.

I can't tell you how many times I wanted to just slap them!!!

What people don't realize is that your mind was free and you were happy, while we live the everyday life of worrying about bills and the struggles of life you had no worries. Whenever I saw you, you were smiling and cracking yourself up. I used to want you to share the joke with me so I can laugh too!! You loved the ocean and marveled about its beauty.

Many of you have looked at her as if Mental Illness is a disease. Mental illness is NOT a disease, it's not something that is contagious, and it's not hereditary though my kids will think it is LOL AND IT'S CERTAINLY NOT A JOKE ALTHOUGH, I JOKE ABOUT IT CAUSE THAT'S HOW I COPE. To me, through everything you have taught me is that life is funny and laughter is therapy.

This is a very thin line between sane and insane. ANYONE CAN CROSS THAT LINE!!! Trust me, now I know it was God's way that I had to see you go through your stages for me to endure my challenges of life.

It was seeing you that kept my head focus, focused for my kids.

I always asked why did you not think about me? Why didn't you stay sane and fight it for me? I asked that question alot in life.

The answer is now very simple to me, because for all I have been through and will continue to go through I NEED TO STAY HAPPY AND STAY SANE FOR MY KIDS! You ARE my guiding light.....

To all who wonder what happen, she can't speak for herself and I can't speak for her, and I too asked the very same question, one thing I can say is TRUE LOVE IS A POWERFUL WEAPON. When used or misused it can strike a dangerous blow. After been dealt with that weapon myself I understand the why, the how, and I now know and understand WHAT happened.....

I am grateful that I got the time to say I love you and in your own way you told me you loved me. I shared the tears with you that flowed when I saw you.

Your tears are my tears now. I can look back now and say you were a good mother, you made me the only mom I know how to be today.

I BRIEFLY had that traditional motherly love from you AND I have always had that daughterly love for you.

MOM I LOVE YOU AND AS BOB WOULD SAY:

"Rise up this mornin',
Smiled with the risin' sun,
Three little birds
Pitch by my doorstep
Singin' sweet songs
Of melodies pure and true,
Sayin', ("This is my message to you")
Singin': "Don't worry 'bout a thing,
*'Cause every little thing gonna be all right." ***

Footnotes: LOL is text speak for Laughing Out Loud. ROTL is text speak for Rolling on the Floor Laughing. **Lyrics by Robert Nester Marley "Three Little Birds" on Album Exodus album released by Bob Marley and the Wailers, 1980.

MY mother and I months before her breakdown.
It's the only picture I have with my mother.

EPILOGUE

Just like the cancer that ended my mother's life, mental illness is a parasite that creeps through your mind and erodes the traits that makes you who you are. It most certainly has had a profound impact on the way my life has turned out; but I am not one to lament. I just thank God that he brought me through all of those situations with my own mind intact – at least I'd like to think that it is. My mother's illness had a monumental impact on every aspect of my life until the day she connected with me in her bedroom and until I had the final release I needed to love and accept myself.

Since her death, I feel as though God has given me a new canvas with which to create the life of my dreams. I have been blessed with new life in my businesses and my entrepreneurial creativity is flowing stronger than ever. I launched my retail store, Let's Journey Into Fashion in 2011 and am happy to say that my clothing has made it to the red carpet. As the stylist for Cyrene Tankard, star of the hit reality TV show *Thicker than Water*. I had the privilege of accompanying her to the Bravo TV premiere of her family's reality show in 2013. It would be the start of an incredible relationship that is expanding into other avenues. I have rebuilt my relationship with God and now realize that without him nothing is possible; and I mean NOTHING! My faith has been restored and I am living my best life so that my kids can live theirs. I have also used my social media platform to empower women who have been voiceless to speak their truths. *I am turning my lemons into some really amazing lemonade and I am watching God do his thing in a much bigger way than I could have ever done on my own.* In just four years since my mother's death, due to a series of blessings from the man above, I was able to share my *Journey Untold*. I hope that this book has touched someone who has suffered silently in his or her own life because of the debilitating and far-reaching effects of mental illness. As this book goes to press, I am in the process of effecting change in my childhood community in the Virgin Islands to revamp the mental health policy and increase support for families. My journey is ever changing, always unfolding in ways I could not predict. It is just turning in a different direction and I hope that as I continue along this path, I can connect with you along the way.

Until we meet again…Yassin.

A Conversation with Yassin S. Hall

Q: Did you view yourself as being different due to your mom's mental illness?

A: While I rather consider myself to be unique with a life that is different from my peers, I did feel confused and odd compared to my classmates. I felt mostly alone and I definitely felt out of place on a daily basis. After a while I just began to think of myself as a unique individual.

Q: Have you ever sought professional treatment to cope with your mom's illness?

A: To this day, and a few therapists later, I refused to speak to anyone about certain aspects of my life until this book. I didn't feel like anyone had a Band-Aid to turn back time and fix her mind, so why bother to open up about it? My first time speaking in public about any of this was at my "Spring into a New YOU" Fashion show in Early 2014. That's when it hit me that if my story can truly help another, then it's meant for me do.

Q: Did you ever blame yourself?

A: As a child I was totally unaware of what mental illness was, so yes, I did blame myself. When the bullies said "I turned my mother crazy" that really hurt to the core of my soul. I mean, how could I deal with that guilt or even begin to process that something I did could have sent my mother off the deep end. I didn't even know how to fix it or if it could be fixed for me to stop doing it to her.

Q: What was it about your mom that embarrassed you most?

A: Hmmm…Oh my, where do I start? Which times? It felt like she would pick the most inopportune times to say or do the most bizarre things when kids who already bullied me were around. I felt like she kept adding fuel to a burning forest fire. If I had to pick just one, it was the time in the high school gym at a basketball game when she walked on to the court and took the ball. She then pointed me out on the bench and told every boy in that gym that they better not think about having sex with me. Then she lifted up her leg while pointing at her private parts. The entire gym laughed. It's funny now, but at that moment all I could do was run home crying on the outside and on the inside.

Q: What was your most memorable moment with and about your mom?

A: What I remember the most is her deep philosophical thoughts about her views on life. She loved Bob Marley's songs and we would sing them together. The most memorable was in her last days battling cancer she spoke to me in her normal voice and in her right mind. She remembered that I lived in Florida and she called me Yassin, after years of 'that girl' or some other variation. It's as if her mind came back for that precious moment in time and she knew me like her daughter; showed concerns for my kids. Then in minutes she was gone again, asking me to leave the room.

Q: What motivated you to write this book at this time in your life?

A: Many have said I should write a book because it will help others; but is wasn't until after my 2014 Spring fashion show that I was in total amazement at the support and love I received after the show. One lady told me I saved her life and gave her hope. On the way to the event, she thought about driving her car in a ditch. She logged onto Instagram, saw my flier and stopped by. She said I gave her the motivation to keep on living.

Q: Did your mom have enough lucid moments as you matured to share how proud of you she was?

A: This brings me tears to answer this question because I've always felt like her possession more than her child. In other words, in her mind, every part of my day belonged solely to her. Up until the time of her death, she never said or showed she was proud of me. I just have to believe she is fine in heaven and looking down proudly at me.

Q: What kind of world did you have to create within and for yourself to help you cope?

A: I was drawn to special places more than just creating a fantasy world. I've always loved the water. It's calming to me. I would draw pictures of boats and the ocean, and just pretend I was at the beach; or I would disappear into my fashion world and sketch designs. I hide myself in my sewing.

Q: Does the impact of your mother's mental illness affect your relationship with men & women? Dating?

A: Yes I'm very selective of who I tell about my life. To gain friendship takes years of just evaluating them to see if they can handle my past without pity or judgments. Are they capable of handling my truth about what is my past life? As for dating it's hard to get really close to men because nothing positive besides my kids have come from sharing my love. In my opinion, many men by default think women are crazy; and most are ignorant in thinking crazy is hereditary. So before even knowing me, they think, "Oh no, her mom is crazy and she could be too. They tend to drift away. If I do get close to anyone, I don't tell them my full truth until I know they are deserving of my truth.

Q: What do you want the readers to get from reading this book?

A: I would like them to see the signs in either themselves or others and get help before it's too late. They should educate their kids about mental illness so they are aware and not cast judgment or bully someone that is different. Instead of teasing, tell your children to lend a hand and be a friend to someone going through stuff.

Q: Are you concerned that you will be made vulnerable by writing the book?

A: I'm concerned that my children and some of my family will be vulnerable because of my revealing the truth. I don't want my kids to be teased about their grandma and targeted to be bullied. I don't want anyone to feel bad for me or pity me. I have lived a good life despite my struggles. To me it's all I have known my life to be. God meant for me to have this life to help others. That is my purpose.

Q: Mental illness is also hereditary and it can affect many members of the same family. Have you seen signs of mental illness in other members of your family?

A: I'm not 100% sure if it's medically confirmed but I have seen irregular behaviors in my family, and from my experience they could use a few sessions on the couch -- including one of my own kids. I am using my experience to encourage them, and provide the tools and information needed to seek help. I have learned that you can't force someone to see that they need help. It is something they have to realize. That's where I play the role of life-mentor. My hope is that they will see the scenarios I've seen, which will trigger them to think, "Hmmm…maybe I should speak to someone."

Q: What is your relationship now with your father? Did you ever mend your differences?

A: After my 2nd sons birth we did develop email and phone communications frequently. After my mother's funeral, I travelled over to St. John to spend the day with him along with my daughter. She is the only one of my four children he has ever met in person. He filled in the gaps to questions I needed the answers too. Sadly my father passed away 1 year and 2 months after that visit from a heart attack. That visit was the last time I saw him alive.

My paternal uncle Samuel H. Hall, Jr. Esq.

ACKNOWLEDGMENTS

I would like to first acknowledge God for giving me this life and the struggles I have encountered. Although it was, and still is hard at times, I see now that my purpose is to help others through my pain. I thank Him for the gift of life. I also extend my gratitude to the following: my family -- My Aunty Ruby, my Godmother Aunty Norma, the Simmonds family, my Uncle Sam, and the best friend God sent me during my trying times in adulthood Jeanelle Moolenaar. I especially want to thank my children Roumell Augustine, Aubrey Warner Jr., Marik Young, and Yamisha Young, for without them I really could not continue to live. I extend additional hugs and kisses to AJ, Riki and Misha for their understanding of the long sleepless nights, and the sacrifices they make every day so we can all try as best as we can to live each other's dreams together.

I would like to thank my co-author Loán Sewer for encouraging me to write my story and also special thanks to her team of editors. Though at the time writing my story about my mother was not my idea my first book, she knew that this story, *Twisted Love*, should be the first in the series of my Journey Untold. She saw the strength and power in this story about my mother's illness. Loán is not only the co-author she is my cousin. She knows my personality and the woman that I have become. She believed in me and knew that together we could make an impact in the community through my experience. Now that it has been brought to fruition, I am humbly grateful for her having taken on this task. Her incredible writing abilities to take out her personal emotions and tell this story with all her soul should be commended. A special thank you to my Grandma Ethlyn Louise Harthman - Lindqvist Hall (RIP) for the gift of land that has been in our family for roughly one hundred and forty-seven years and my home in St. John. I will forever treasure my homeland. Lastly, my thanks to the Virgin Islands community for their outpouring of support and continued love. I thank you sincerely, for without my community I really would not be this strong version of ME today.

ABOUT THE AUTHORS

Yassin S. Hall

(pronounced Yah Seen) She comes from humble beginnings that would make most people throw in the towel, but her journey is one that demonstrates how important perseverance and determination are to reaching one's destiny. She's a mother, dance mom, fashionista, model manager, entrepreneur, life mentor, speaker and now Author. She is Yassin Hall, a U.S. Virgin Islander with roots on St. Thomas and St. John. However, Hall's true passion has always been tied to fashion and clothing, as she began modeling in her teen years and designing.

From the age of twelve, she was raised by her maternal grandmother and paternal uncle after her mother suffered a mental breakdown in front of her. It was a day that changed her life forever. She wants her story as a child living with a mother with mental illness to raise awareness and help others. Mental illness in many communities is taboo & unspoken. She feels that cycle should be broken so others suffering with depression, anxiety, and mental disorders can be made aware of their conditions and know that it is okay to receive help before going over the edge.

Follow Yassin on Twitter: @journeyuntold

Loán C. Sewer

Loán (pronounced Lo'an) Sewer is a prolific writer and speaker, published author, and strategic marketer whose work spans the journalism, marketing, advertising, and public relations arenas. She has developed compelling content and dynamic marketing strategies that have yielded favorable results for companies and non-profit organizations in a multitude of industries such as Turner Construction, Control Risks, The National Urban League, The Virgin Islands Department of Tourism, The West Indian Company Limited, and a member of the U.S. House of Representatives. Loán is also a co-founder of The USVI Alliance, Inc., a non-profit organization based in the Washington, D.C. area that promotes the importance of the U.S. Virgin Islands diaspora in the territory's economic revitalization and reform. Her writing has been featured in the anthology *Tears to Triumph: Women Learn to Live, Love, & Thrive* and currently writes a popular bi-weekly column, "Jewels of the Virgin Isles," in the *Virgin Islands Source*, an online daily newspaper in the U.S. Virgin Islands. Loán is the founder of Gobi (Go-Bee) Consulting, LLC, a marketing and communications consulting firm based in Maryland and St. Thomas, U.S. Virgin Islands. She is a proud alumna of the University of Maryland at College Park where she received her B.A. in Journalism and Temple University where she received her Masters degree in Tourism and Hospitality Management.

Follow Loán on Twitter: @LoTalksTourism